The Clue Phone's Ringing ... It's for You!

Healing Humor for Women Divorcing

By
Christine K. Clifford

Illustrated by Jack Lindstrom

Published by:-

Anshan Ltd
11a Little Mount Sion
Tunbridge Wells
Kent. TN1 1YS

Tel: +44 (0) 1892 557767
Fax: +44 (0) 1892 530358
e-mail: info@anshan.co.uk
web site: www.anshan.co.uk

© 2012 Christine K. Clifford

ISBN: 978 1 848290 65 5

All rights reserved. No part of this publication may be reproduced, stored in a retrieval system, or transmitted in any form or by any means, electronic, mechanical, photocopying, recording or otherwise, without the prior written permission of the publisher.

The use of registered names, trademarks, etc, in this publication does not imply, even in the absence of a specific statement that such names are exempt from the relevant laws and regulations and therefore for general use.

While every effort has been made to ensure the accuracy of the information contained within this publication, the publisher can give no guarantee for information about drug dosage and application thereof contained in this book. In every individual case the respective user must check current indications and accuracy by consulting other pharmaceutical literature and following the guidelines laid down by the manufacturers of specific products and the relevant authorities in the country in which they are practicing.

British Library Cataloguing in Publication Data

A catalogue record for this book is available from the British Library.

Editor: Tara Foss
Cover Design: Graham Rich
Cover and internal cartoons: Jack Lindstrom
Typeset by: Kerry Press Ltd, UK
Printed in the USA by:

DEDICATION:

This book is dedicated to Nancy Van Dyken and Pat Miles Zimmerman,
who never let go of my hand, and
to Amber Serwat, who helped me find my inner Diva.

Testimonials

"I love this book! *The Clue Phone's Ringing* has much to offer not only divorcing women, but most importantly– to women in abusive relationships. Christine's clarity about her process, her struggle, her learning will be such a gift to women out there. More importantly, I know of no other book that has been able to bring some level of humor to women in abusive relationships. The ability of my clients to learn to laugh at hardships is so healing. Christine's book provides hope that there is a better future for them."

– Nancy VanDyken, Licensed Psychologist, L.I.C. Social Worker, Author of *Forgive Him? Are You Kidding? Preparing Your Heart to Forgive*

P.S. This should be required reading for counselors, psychologists, social workers, and anyone doing therapy. I believe this book would be helpful in women's shelters; certainly I will recommend it to my clients of abuse at some point in their therapy process, to women just starting the dating process again and also to colleagues of mine. Good work. I look forward to seeing it in print.

"Christine isn't just a Divorcing Diva, she's also the inventor of something that Alexander Graham Bell may have invented instead of the standard telephone if he had thought of it–*The Clue Phone*! The great thing about The Clue Phone is that it doesn't have any breakable parts, needs no batteries and never needs replacing. All you have to do is listen! The old stigma was that if someone was married and divorced more than once, they were probably a bad bet. The new idea is that they are probably someone who, like me, now happily married for the first time for more than a decade–the fifth time around for me– believes that life is too precious to spend in unbearable matrimony even if those circumstances are simply a wrong match. And yet, I believe in the sacred bonds of a legal/spiritual union rather than just picking up with someone. I believe in true love and the search to find it even if it means being 'that woman who's been

Testimonials

divorced-'how many times'? I think that more women need *The Clue Phone*, and now, thankfully, Christine has invented it. Read on ...."
- Acharya Sri Khadi Madama Author of *Finding Shangri La: Seven Yoga Principles for Creating Success & Happiness*

"What a fabulous read! We do need to see humor through divorce, and *The Clue Phone* reminds us that it's OK! I found myself glued to every page. Now that I'm going through my third divorce, when the Clue Phone rang, I picked it up ...listened ...gathered information, and moved on. Thank you, Christine, for putting this on paper for others to read"
–Dorothy Benham, Miss America 1977, Opera Singer

"A story from the heart about healing a broken heart. Christine's honest telling of a shocking story is an inspiration."
– Dr. Vicki Rackner, Author of *Caregiving Without Regrets*, CNN Health Advisor

"I really love Christine's book. It's a fast, upbeat read that many women can identify with ... unfortunately. I got a real feeling of feminine solidarity from it — which is a very healthy direction for women to go in. The 'Sisterhood' vibe of sharing awful relationships, laughing at how ridiculously bad they are, hopefully forewarning others, but then gathering strength and independence with other women is empowering. I like the encouraging, learning/warning, affirming message of *The Clue Phone*, and think it will be a comfort to all Divorcing Divas!"
– Dr. Mary Harlow, Licensed Psychologist

Contents

Acknowledgements	ix
Introduction	1
Nothing to Laugh About	5
The Man of My Dreams	7
The Love Story	10
The Clue Phone's Ringing Off the Hook!	14
A Marriage Made in Hell	16
Nothing a Little Alcohol Can't Cure!	19
Someone Saved My Life Today	23
Finally, The End	25
Divorcing Diva	28
The Games People Play	31
"I See," Says the Blind Woman	36
Great Day to Be Alive …	38
Keep On Movin' On! Top Ten Tips for Divorcing Divas	42
You Might Be a Divorcing Diva If …	45
Taking the High Road	112
Remove Foot from Mouth	125
Don't Forget to Laugh!	129
Resources Page	131
And Now For Some Unsolicited Advice: Moving Forward Into the Great Unknown	135
About the Author	139
About the Illustrator	141
About Divorcing Divas®	142
About The Cancer Club®	144
Other Books by Christine Clifford	146

Acknowledgements

It has been said that during times of adversity, you learn who your friends are, and you learn who your friends aren't. Having been through a few of life's biggest challenges (a diagnosis of breast cancer in 1994, and two divorces), I feel pretty darn blessed.

I would like to thank my first husband for twenty-nine years of marriage and the gift of my two sons. I thank him for accepting the end of our marriage graciously, kindly, and without conflict. And I thank him—and his family—for remaining my friend.

I would like to thank my sons, Tim and Brooks, and Tim's partner Chris, for putting up with their "crazy" Mom, who puts her life out there for all the world to see. They've always been there supporting me, loving me, and laughing along the way. I hope I don't embarrass you too much.

My brothers Greg and James Meyer and extraordinary step-mom Stephanie Meyer have dried a lot of tears. Thank you.

I am deeply grateful to Shan and Andrew White, and Anshan Ltd. for believing in me and publishing this book and Tara Foss for her editorial input.

I want to thank my best friends Pat and Bucky Zimmerman, who listen, offer advice and a shoulder, and who didn't let me fall down a hole, when I was teetering on the edge. Thanks for never letting go, and always being here for me.

I am eternally grateful to Nancy Van Dyken, for helping me see my life for what it had become, and where it could go.

The friends who have stood by me through thick and thin (even when I'm golfing poorly): Virginia and Bob Carlson, Cheryl Sandeen, Kathy and Pat Lewis, Parrel Caplan, Dawn and Jon Earl, Jean Golden, Lori Frank, Aija and Tom Meehan, Gail Tilsner, Gregg Egginton, Jennifer Shirley and Bruce Hazen, Tracy Stewart, Sue Bleecker, Bev Blize Nickerson, Marian

Acknowledgements

and Dan O'Neil, Tom Schmidt, Jeff Lillemoe, Isaac Diaz, Jeff Evans, Jim Greer, Jan Moore, Adele Brellenthin, Sally and Bill Hall, Barb Demos, CJ Dube, Steve Schussler and Sunhi Ryan, Lauren and Merle Shapiro (and all the fabulous women of The Full Moon), Mary Barker, Mary Harlow, Mary McNutt, Michaelyn Born, Michael Collins, Randy Segal, Stacy Andresen, and Vicki Rackner.

I'm eternally grateful to Annie Child and Susan Stryker for selling my house in six days.

A special thanks to Barb Greenberg, who met me as a total stranger for a cup of coffee, and walked away a friend for life. Thank you for helping launch Divorcing Divas, and for being one of my very best friends.

To all the Divorcing Divas and our supporters: Susan Garfield, Karen Stafford, Jessie Welf, Joelle Pink, Michelle Palmer, Kim Rauser, Paul Wilkenson, Sharon Hall, Linda Margl, Alison Nelson, Melinda Bonk, Christina Boyd, Barbara Bencini, Jeanne Rosengren, Gary Hansen, Linda Olup, Morrie Wagner, Diana Pierce, Deb Hopp, Carla Beaurline, Lisa Wohlfert, Kristin Harper, and all of our sponsors, vendors, volunteers, and attendees of our events. Thank you for your support!

But most of all, I want to thank Amber Serwat, who has made me laugh and cry as we brain-stormed on what truly makes a Divorcing Diva. You are a sister, a best friend, and a colleague.

God has blessed me with good health, a strong faith, a loving family, an abundance of friends, a passion for creativity, a vision of purpose, and the gift of life and laughter. Remember: It's not the end … it's the beginning!

Introduction

The phone was ringing off the hook.

Not the iPhone in my pocket. Not the AT&T cordless in my office. The one in my head.

We had only known each other for three months, but were already madly in love and engaged. But more on that in a minute.

Mr. Wonderful, as we'll call him, had to go out of the country for several days and asked if I would watch his cat. On the day of his departure, I arrived around 5:00pm and made the long walk down the corridor of his apartment complex. Arriving at #1917, I glanced up and stared in amazement: yellow warning tape was criss-crossing the white door, and there was an "EVICTION NOTICE" taped across the peek-hole.

"Eviction notice?" I thought to myself. "What is that?! Isn't that one of those things that they use to throw people out of their place?" I looked at the door, looked at the key, looked at the door, looked at the key.

I sat down in the hallway in front of the door and pulled out my cell. His adorable cat was meowing loudly on the other side.

Thankfully, I got a hold of Mr. Wonderful in India, and told him what I was looking at. "Oh, those Xo#X!?/@z! people in the office! They must have lost my rent check again! I used to date someone in the office, and she loves to screw with me now. Honey, will you do me a favor? Can you go down and pay my rent? I'll pay you back as soon as I get back in the country. Thanks, sweetheart. I love you so much!"

The Clue Phone was starting to ring ...

Introduction

I slowly stood up, and made my way back down the hall to the elevator and went down to the office. Mr. Wonderful wasn't one month behind on his rent—he was *three* months behind on his rent! Paying the bill, I remember to this day thinking, "This does *not* feel good."

But Mr. Wonderful came back from his travels and promptly wrote me a check to cover the one I had written on his behalf. "Oh, those Xo#X!?/@z! people in the office!" I thought to myself. It can't possibly be *him*.

Nothing to Laugh About

"Learning to laugh at trouble radically increases the amount of things there are to laugh at."

– Author Unknown

I cannot pinpoint the exact moment when humor became a purposeful part of my therapy as I recovered from my second divorce. Looking back, there were moments so absurd, that if I couldn't laugh about them, I'd cry. And certainly laughter feels better than tears.

I learned about the healing power of laughter going through a journey that felt somewhat similar: facing and fighting breast cancer in 1994. The feelings of anger, fear, denial, and grief parallel that experience, and yet somehow humor managed to find me everywhere I looked as I endured ten months of chemotherapy, a month of radiation, surgeries, and the loss of my hair. The only difference was that one was a struggle for my breast. The other was a struggle for my heart.

There is nothing humorous about getting divorced. At the age of eighteen my father took me, my two brothers, and my sister out to dinner to our favorite restaurant in Pasadena. Over popovers with jam and rare prime rib, he informed us he was leaving our mother. The next year was a blur as he sold the house on Winston Avenue that we'd lived in all our lives, moved with my youngest brother James into a neighboring community, and set me, my sister Pam, and Mom up in a tiny house on Bradbury Road. Greg was already off at college.

Mom never had to face the stigma and shame of being a divorcee in the 1970s. She died of breast cancer at the age of 42 before their divorce became final. I remember thinking, "That will *never* happen to me." I would dream of sitting on the front porch of my house with the white picket fence, seven grandchildren playing in my backyard with our four dogs and two cats, while my husband of sixty years and I would be sipping banana daiquiris.

The Clue Phone's Ringing

Funny how life has other plans ...

The Man of My Dreams

*"No one knows how it is that with one glance
a boy can break through into a girl's heart."*

– Nancy Thayer

I couldn't wait to get out of that tiny house on Bradbury and go off to college to pursue a life of academia, sports, friendships, and causes. I joined a sorority, Delta Gamma, my freshman year at the University of Denver, and promptly became the "Sweetheart of Beta Theta Pi."

Throwing myself into dating—a hobby I was good at—I was having a heck of a great time when the Betas invited me to serve as Hostess at a Beta 100 Year Reunion. "You'll be the only girl there, Christine," they explained, as the event was open to "Men Only." No wives, no girlfriends.

"Can we count on you to play Hostess?" they asked. "Play Hostess? How many men are you expecting?" I inquired. "Oh, about 200."

"I'm all in! *That's* what we're talking about!" I squealed in delight. My mind was spinning with possibilities!

The night of the event, a camel color, long sleeve dress with a huge scoop neckline draped my body and definitely showed off my assets. Showing up early, I greeted each man at the door as they started to file in to the fraternity house. Large ones, small ones, short ones, tall ones, men of all ages filled the foyer and spilled into the living room. As the night wore on, I decided I had greeted every man in attendance, when suddenly I saw *him* from across the crowded room.

The Clue Phone's Ringing

"That's the man I'm going to marry," I said to myself.

He must have thought the same thing as he worked his way through the crowd to meet me. We started dating immediately, and truth be told, we were almost never apart for close to thirty-three years. Twenty-nine of those years we were married, as I moved half-way across the country from California to Minnesota, and we produced two beautiful and wonderful sons. We had years of joy and happiness, lots of friends and fun hobbies that we loved to share.

But there was a fatal flaw in our marriage: by default, I became the primary breadwinner. That would have been OK, if we had made the decision together. But as our kids were born, and we needed a bigger house, hockey skates, cars, and tuition, the harder I worked, the less he did. It was a joke to a lot of our friends and family, but for me, there was deep and growing resentment.

"Why couldn't *I* be the one staying home with the kids?" I thought, as I'd board another plane for my umpteenth business trip. "Why can't *I* be the one taking them to baseball practice, and going to school plays, and teaching them how to drive?" But by that time, my career had become all-consuming. And my husband? His golf handicap was almost scratch.

After begging and pleading with him to take more responsibility—especially after the diagnosis with breast cancer— the truth became evident: he just didn't have it in him. Within weeks of my 50th birthday, a decision was made: I would get a divorce. It was too much to bear the anger and resentment that had built up all those years.

My divorce to my first husband could probably serve as the standard to which all divorces should be compared. My husband didn't even get an attorney. Our divorce was finalized in four months. We actually remained living in our house, on separate floors, until we sold it almost six months later.

Today, he and his girlfriend have me over with our sons and my former in-laws for Thanksgiving, and I reciprocate at mine. Looking back on that marriage, I tell myself, "We had a lot of fun. We raised two fabulous boys, and we're still friends." I still love him—he's a good man. I'm just not "in love" with him. And I've never regretted my decision to leave.

The Love Story

*"Love is not blind—it sees more, not less.
But because it sees more, it is willing to see less."*

– Julius Gordon

My second marriage begins—and ends—with a love story.

Within weeks of making my decision to divorce Husband #1, I met "Mr. Wonderful." It wasn't a "chance" meeting or our destiny to find each other. I actually went looking for him.

Writing a book about sales, and having already found a publisher, I was almost through with the book when I started to think, "Who should write the cover testimonial that will propel it to the top of the Best Sellers' Lists? Possibly my friend Harvey Mackay, author of *Swim with the Sharks Without Being Eaten Alive*? Maybe Jeffrey Gitomer (*Little Red Book of Selling*) or Seth Godin, both best-selling authors of their own sales books? Ah-ha! I've got it: Mr. Wonderful!"

Mr. Wonderful was a successful author, and in fact, I had given a copy of one of his books to my sales force at The SPAR Group—a marketing services company I worked for out of New York for fifteen years, back when I was employed in the corporate world. I immediately started networking all over the country to see if any of my colleagues or acquaintances knew Mr. Wonderful and could make an introduction. Everyone knew *of* him, but no one knew him personally. "Oh, he writes fabulous books!" they'd say. "But I've never seen him or heard him."

The Love Story

In the midst of this search, my dreams were answered: a purple flier landed in the mailbox that said that Mr. Wonderful was going to be the keynote speaker in Portland, Oregon! My best friend from college lived in Portland, and we hadn't seen each other for ten years. Plus, I'd never been to Portland. "Perfect," I thought. "I'll fly off to Portland, get an introduction and ask him to write the Foreword to my book!"

I flew to Oregon and on the morning of his speech, I showed up bright and early so I wouldn't miss my chance of meeting him. Walking in to the auditorium, I noticed a handful of people standing down by the stage. Approaching, someone I knew said, "Christine, what are *you* doing in Portland?"

"I came to meet Mr. Wonderful," was my response.

"Really? Because he's right here! Let me introduce you."

We chatted briefly as I was cognizant of the fact that he was getting ready to go on stage and may need some time to collect his thoughts for his presentation. I told him that I had flown half way across the country to meet him, and wanted to talk to him about writing the Foreword to a book I was writing.

"Great," he said, handing me his business card. "Why don't you give me a call next week?"

Glancing at the card, I burst into laughter. It turned out he lived less than ten miles away from me in Minneapolis. "Too perfect," I said. "I'll call you next week to set up a meeting."

I stayed to hear him speak. He was a fabulous presenter and got two standing ovations from the crowd. Fans rushed the stage when he was finished, hoping he would autograph their books. Slipping out of the conference when he was done, I spent the rest of the weekend with my best friend Jennifer and her husband Bruce. On Sunday night, they dropped me off at the airport.

The Clue Phone's Ringing

I'm a firm believer that everything happens for a reason. For some reason, and by pure coincidence, I ended up sitting across the aisle from Mr. Wonderful in First Class. At first, he seemed preoccupied as I tried to make small talk and compliment him on his speech. He then took off his glasses, put down the *New York Times* crossword puzzle, and started a conversation.

All the way home we laughed and chatted. At one point, he actually swung his legs over the armrest of his chair and was kicking his feet like a little boy full of excitement. When our plane landed, he followed me down to baggage claim. He hadn't checked any bags.

I told him I would call him for lunch. So, Wednesday it was, at my country club, only moments from his apartment. We started our lunch at 11:30am. We were still at lunch at 11:30pm. Only lunch had morphed into bottles of wine, and then dinner.

He suddenly looked at his watch and exclaimed, "Oh my! I have a 7:00am flight to Atlanta in the morning. I have to go." By the time I drove back to my house, an email was waiting for me. By the time I woke up the next morning, he had left a voicemail.

He was going to be out of town for five days, but we talked for hours on the phone every day. The day he was getting back, I was leaving to go out of town for five days myself. More conversations. The first day we were both going to be home was Valentine's Day.

"Great!" I said. "How about if I come over and cook you breakfast?"

The Love Story

That morning, looking around my kitchen, I scratched my head. Now mind you, I had been in a thirty-three year relationship with my first husband. I wasn't used to dating! I didn't know if Mr. Wonderful would even have pots and pans. So I brought everything with me but the kitchen sink!

I showed up at his apartment at 9:00am. At 9:07, he asked me to marry him.

I said, "Yes."

The Clue Phone's Ringing Off the Hook!

"The world will never starve for want of wonder."

– Gilbert Keith Chesterton

Who knows why I said, "Yes, I will marry you" to a man I barely knew. I was used to "love at first sight;" after all, that's what had happened with my first husband. I was used to being a "wife," and couldn't imagine dating in my 50s. I'd been out of practice for so long!

Perhaps I was swept up in the fantasy of who I perceived Mr. Wonderful to be: a successful author and speaker; funny, charming, and a good conversationalist. Little did I know what lurked ahead for me.

It had taken me six months to sell my house, and now it was time to move in with my fiancé. Husband #1 had found a new girlfriend, and he was ready to move on as well. Calculating what Mr. Wonderful had spent in rent for the past six years at his high-rise apartment, I begged him to go looking for houses with me. For one thing, I had a house full of furniture. For another, I didn't want to take the capital gains hit on my taxes.

His complete rejection and many objections to looking for a house seemed strange, but again, it never occurred to me: *The Clue Phone was ringing ...*

Finally, with my home closing only weeks away and the fact that I couldn't get Mr. Wonderful to look at a single house, there was no choice but to move in with him to the high rise. He had a place full of furniture, too, so I frantically put all of mine up in an estate sale. My family's Steinway

The Clue Phone's Ringing Off the Hook!

grand piano. My treadmill for those snowy days in Minneapolis. My beloved collection of holiday decorations. I sold it all and moved in with Mr. Wonderful.

He waited three months before he told me the news: he hadn't paid his taxes in two years, and now he was going in to year three without any estimates paid. He was hundreds of thousands of dollars in debt. It had never occurred to me to run a credit check on him. If I had, I would have learned why he didn't want to go shopping for houses: he had no credit!

Not wanting to start a marriage where money was an issue, I offered to help him pay off his taxes with the money I had just earned selling my house.

We no sooner got his taxes paid, when his second ex-wife (I was soon to be #3—*large* Clue Phone there, mind you!) sued him for $225,000 in unpaid child support and alimony. She won her case, but her only recourse at that time was to have him put in jail. I guess she figured that having him out making a living was better than having him doing nothing in jail.

The Clue Phone's Ringing ... It's for You!

Three months later, we got married.

A Marriage Made in Hell

"It is not what he has, nor even what he does, which directly expresses the worth of a man, but what he is."

– Henri Frederic Amiel

It was shortly after we got married that the abuse started. The first time was shocking, really. We had just returned from a business trip of mine to Orlando, Florida where I had introduced Mr. Wonderful to some dear friends and colleagues. One of our activities was playing a round of golf with my friend, the CEO of a large Orlando hospital. Mr. Wonderful's behavior on the golf course was so atrocious—throwing clubs, swearing, not finishing a hole—that I was angry and embarrassed.

On the plane ride home, Mr. Wonderful consumed two full bottles of wine. He was so inebriated that as he left the plane, he grabbed the flight attendant that had been serving him and gave her a kiss on the lips. I was, of course, disgusted.

When we got back to our apartment after the long flight home in total silence, I told him I had been embarrassed about his behavior. With that, he grabbed my cosmetic bag and started racing toward our balcony. All of my womanly possessions were in that bag, and it was over my dead body that he was going to throw it overboard from the 24th floor. As I grabbed it from him, pulling it back inside the apartment, he turned and pushed me down on the floor, crash landing on top of me and the bag. I had a broken thumb.

He stood up and stared down on me crying and clutching my thumb and said, "You don't *possibly* think I was going to throw that over the railing now, *did you?*"

I spent the night locked in our laundry room, too frightened of what he might do next.

A Marriage Made in Hell

The next morning, he couldn't have been more remorseful or loving. He apologized profusely, and I remember thinking, "Well, he *was* drunk. Maybe it was an accident."

The next time, it was a broken rib when he again crashed down on me with all his weight while having sex. But it was the mouthwash incident that really took the cake.

YouTube™ had just launched on the internet, and Mr. Wonderful was pretty enthralled. He'd often call me over to watch a certain video with him, and we both got a big kick out of people, babies, and animals doing silly and strange things.

One night, clicking on YouTube™ and scanning the history of the videos he had watched, I came across one that said, "Sandra Bullock." Hmm, I pondered. "I wonder what a video of Sandra Bullock might be about?" It was a beautiful montage of photos of the actress, all PG-rated, and in rapid succession.

That night, sitting on the toilet while Mr. Wonderful was brushing his teeth, I teased, "Watched a little Sandra Bullock video, did we?"

"No, I didn't." he shot back quickly and firmly.

"Well, you did, honey, because it was on the history of the videos you watched."

"NO, I DIDN'T!" he exclaimed loudly.

"Well, honey, it's OK that you did. She's a pretty lady." With that, he picked up a brand new quart of mouthwash we'd just purchased at the drug store that day, walked over to me on the toilet, and poured the entire thing over my head.

The mouthwash splashed everywhere: the walls, the floor, the vanity, completely wiping out the roll of toilet paper. Making a decision that I was never going to clean it up, I just waited to see if *he* ever would.

Our cleaning people—a wonderful couple who were in their 70s—cleaned the floor that week, as they always did. My guess is that they never looked up on the walls. Because a year or so later when we actually did buy a house and moved out of the high rise, while packing the last things out of that bathroom, I glanced at the walls. The tint of the blue mouthwash could still be seen.

Nothing a Little Alcohol Can't Cure!

> *"The measure of success is not whether you have a tough problem to deal with, but whether it's the same problem you had last year."*
>
> – John Foster Dulles

His drinking had become atrocious, and his two older sons were begging me to intervene. They had already spoken to his sister and brother-in-law. They were all willing to fly to Minnesota. He was having blackouts and passing out—full dinner conversations would be totally forgotten the next morning. And he was losing everything but the kitchen sink. Passports, driver's licenses, credit cards, keys: if it wasn't attached to his body, he'd lose it.

One time three other couples—among my closest friends—Mr. Wonderful, and I took a trip to Santa Fe, New Mexico to celebrate one couple's first wedding anniversary. We had all gone out to dinner, and were sitting around a big round table. The rabbi who had married the couple in Santa Fe the year before just happened to show up, and we gleefully invited him to join us.

The conversation was flowing and everyone was having a fabulous time. Suddenly, one of the other men turned to Mr. Wonderful and said, "Mr. Wonderful, what do you think?"

I stared in horror as I saw Mr. Wonderful's face plopped in the food on his dinner plate. I shook him hard, and he slowly sat up. Food was dripping off his face, and down his shirt. My girlfriends snapped their fingers and said, "Chris, *come here.*" They hauled me in to the ladies' room.

The Clue Phone's Ringing

"You have *got* to leave this guy, Christine!" I responded, "I know. But he really needs to get into treatment." We all loaded him in the car, where he passed out again. As we pulled up to the casita where we were staying, one of the men asked me, "What do you want to do with him?"

"Just leave him here," I said. He stayed passed out in the car all night.

At this point, we had purchased our dream home, with me putting up 100% of our down payment. By now I had helped him gain a decent credit rating by paying all of his bills on time, so we put his name on the mortgage along with mine. He'd make compelling arguments that since he made more money than I did, he should put *his* money into *our* retirement program: *His* SEP IRA.

It was a Friday afternoon when Mr. Wonderful figured out that he had accidently double-booked himself for two speeches on the same day: one in Las Vegas and the other in the Bahamas. Having already purchased both sets of airline tickets for the two of us to travel to both locations, he was furious at himself.

Leaving a voicemail message on the phone service of his client in the Bahamas, he canceled his upcoming appearance, only weeks away. I was upset because I felt he should have waited to discuss this with someone over the phone on Monday, rather than leave a voicemail with such terrible news.

On Saturday, while sitting in the lower level of our house watching his college football team on TV, a message came through the fax machine. It was the group in the Bahamas: they were suing him for $25,000 for breach of contract.

"Honey, we can't possibly pay this! We have to do something!" I implored. "In fact, I've been thinking about this all night. Here are a couple of suggestions: why don't we contact both groups and see if one of them will have *me* come and speak instead? I won't even charge them for my appearance!"

"They don't want *you*, for God's sake! *I'm* the famous one," he spouted, finishing up the last drops of a full bottle of wine. It was only 3:00pm in the afternoon.

"OK. Here's another suggestion," I said. "What if you call up the group in the Bahamas and offer to do two, or maybe even three events, for the price of one?"

And in the middle of that sentence, sitting two feet away from him on the couch, **BOOM!!!**

He hit me square in the middle of my face.

I had definitely passed out, because when I came to the first words out of my mouth were, "Did I just fall off the roof of our house?"

I actually felt like someone had taken me like a rag doll and slammed my head against the pavement. Looking down, realizing I was bleeding, I started to scream, "You alcoholic! You ass-hole, get out of the house! Get out of the house!"

His oldest son, who had been living with us for several months and was part of TEAM INTERVENTION, could hear me screaming all the way up in his bedroom on the fourth floor of our house. Bounding down the stairs, he took one look at me and started screaming at his dad.

The next week, I asked Mr. Wonderful if he would willingly go for an evaluation of his drinking. He enthusiastically agreed. In fact, I'm convinced he thought the person doing the evaluation would look him square in the eye and say, "Mr. Wonderful, you don't have a drinking problem."

The psychiatrist looked at him after the end of a three hour session and said, "I have your diagnosis. We've had a long day. Would you like to come back?"

Mr. Wonderful looked at him and said, "No, go ahead and tell me what you think."

"You're a severe alcoholic," he said. "I highly recommend you begin treatment immediately."

Someone Saved My Life Today

*"I have no Yesterdays,
Time took them away;
Tomorrow may not be—
But I have today."*

– Pearl Yeadon McGinnis

Mr. Wonderful never went to treatment. He, like many alcoholics, believed he was "special" and that he could simply treat himself. He'd make the argument that he didn't work well in "groups." He said he knew what his problems were and would fix them.

He quit drinking, for a year. Cold turkey. Of course, he blamed me for his shaking hands, telling me I made him anxious. But then the verbal abuse started, stronger and more powerful than before.

"Honey, I'm going to the grocery store," he'd say. "Do we need anything?"

Opening the refrigerator, I'd respond, "Yes, we could use some Peach Snapple® (my beverage of choice)."

"*WE* could use some Peach Snapple®, Chris?" he'd start off sarcastically.

"Yes, we could use some Peach Snapple®," I'd answer again.

"*WE* could use some Peach Snapple®, Chris?"

"Oh, I'm sorry, Mr. Wonderful. *I* could use some Peach Snapple®."

We saw a brilliant psychologist, a woman whom Mr. Wonderful's regular psychologist had recommended we see for his ADHD assessment. We saw her as a couple four times, both filling out extensive questionnaires relative to his behavior. On the fourth session, she offered us several suggestions and courses of action. We thanked her, left her office, and made an appointment to see his therapist.

That afternoon, my cell phone rang. It was the psychologist we'd just seen. "Hi, Christine. I am terribly concerned for you. I believe you're in a relationship that is very abusive, from all that you've shared with me and from the patterns that I observed in our joint sessions. As is true in the abusive dynamic, I don't recommend couples therapy. In fact, I am not willing to do it because I'm afraid the session, as is often the case with abuse, only becomes another avenue to abuse you. As is true with abusive men, I experienced in our sessions mean, cruel, narcissistic, and uncaring behavior."

I took a deep breath. This was the first time I felt validated. I wasn't crazy after all.

She continued, "Since he is not my client, I will not be following him. However, I am very concerned about you. Abuse is a difficult dynamic and recovery is possible. So if you're open to it, I would like to see you."

"See *me*? Oh, my God," I thought. "What did *I* do? Call him names?" I made the appointment, filled with fear and anxiety. When I walked in, she handed me a book called *The Verbally Abusive Relationship* by Patricia Evans. I burst into tears. "Did I call him an 'asshole' in front of you, Doctor?"

She handed me a box of tissues, and said, "Christine, you don't even see it. You don't even *know* how deeply your mind has been toyed with. Abuse is a slow form of brainwashing, and women don't even realize when it is going on. Over time, they lose trust in themselves and their own wisdom, and struggle to know who they really are versus what they are told they are. They normalize the abuse."

I saw that psychologist on my own for almost a year. At one point, as I was getting closer and closer to ending the marriage, Mr. Wonderful actually drove over to her office and left an envelope for her. When I came for my next appointment, since I was her client, not him, she showed me the envelope with an eight-page, single-spaced letter and recommended we don't even address it because it would only be more abuse in writing, rather than verbally. She held it up, unread, and said, "We don't really want to read this, do we?" And with that, she handed it to me to do with as I wished. I took it home, went out to my driveway and burned it, unread, and watched the ashes go up in smoke.

Finally, The End

"Faith is an act of rational choice which determines us to act as if certain things were true and in the confident expectation that they will prove to be true."

– William R. Inge

It was only a few weeks later that things came to an end.

Invited to play golf at 11:00am on a Sunday with two of my friends with whom we had traveled to Santa Fe, I begged them to let Mr. Wonderful join us to make a foursome. "I have to work the previous two days, and he'll be really angry if I take another weekend day without him."

"Only if he behaves, Chris," implored my friend. "He's such a mess on the golf course. It isn't fun for anyone." I promised he would (knowing he wouldn't) and thanked them profusely.

The two days and nights before, I had been working hard and was exhausted. I had a client in from out of town, and had been in meetings from dawn to dusk. On Saturday night, like every night—365 days of the year—Mr. Wonderful wanted to have sex.

"I can't do it tonight, I'm exhausted," I said. I could feel the anger in his voice and his body as he leapt out of bed and started heading toward the door.

"And honey, can you do me a *huge* favor, please, in the morning?" I asked, as he walked out of the room. "Do you think you could let me sleep in? Our tee-time isn't until 11:00."

When Mr. Wonderful finally came back to bed he, of course, woke me up. It was 2:00am. I managed to fall back asleep, but then it was 6:00am when he got up, turned the lights on in the bathroom and started taking his shower. Sleep in? By this time, I'm wide awake! He proceeds to blow dry his hair, use the electric toothbrush, and then starts heading out the door when he realizes I'm watching him.

The Clue Phone's Ringing

Coming over to the side of my bed, he put his hands on each of my upper arms and started bouncing me up and down saying, "Chrissy, Chrissy, Chrissy. *You* can go back to sleep." He let go, and scooting out the other side of the bed where he couldn't touch me, I pronounced, "You are *not* playing golf with us today!"

"Good, because I don't like to play anyway!" And he was gone.

I tried to call him later that morning to apologize for cutting him out of the golf game. No answer. I left another message right before we teed-off. Telling my friends the story, they both looked at me on the golf course and said, "Chris, *what on earth* are you apologizing to *him* for? He's abusive! Stop calling him!"

I tried one last time. Arriving home that evening, I was greeted all right: by a seven day silent treatment. After the first day, I approached Mr. Wonderful and said, "It's been 24 hours since we last spoke. Do you think we could talk about what happened?"

"Nope."

"It's been 48 hours since we last spoke. Do you think we could talk about what happened?" I tried again.

"Nope."

I tried one more time after 72 hours. On the fourth day, walking in to our bedroom, finding him watching TV, I said, "Honey, it's been four days since we've spoken. Do you think we could talk about what happened?"

"Nope," he said one more time, without even as much as a glance.

Finally, The End

I don't know if God was watching over me that night, or if it was my Guardian Angel. I just knew he had violated my Drama-Free Zone for the last time. I took one last look at him, and I was done. "I could be happier living in a $400 a month apartment down on Hennepin Avenue than I am being married to this man, living in this house," I thought. I turned and walked out of the room. The next morning, I called my attorney.

I said that my second marriage begins, and ends, with a love story. The end of the story is that I decided it was time for me to start loving myself again.

Divorcing Diva

"And then the day came when the risk to remain tight in a bud was more painful than the risk it took to blossom."

– Anais Nin

Looking back now and with therapy, time, and introspection I see how I justified staying in that marriage: I couldn't imagine being a two-time divorcee! I loved his four kids, and they had already been through so much. I thought, "If he'd just go through treatment, maybe things could be different." And there's my triple AAA+++ caregiver personality: it was my destiny to take care of others!

What I've learned going through two divorces, however, is that divorce is still a very difficult subject for most people to discuss. In fact, when my parents were going through their divorce almost forty years ago, the kids in my family weren't even allowed to *say* the word "divorce."

We had to call it their "separation" or their "situation."

Too bad my parents weren't intuitive enough to trademark those words, "The Situation." Mike "The Situation" Sorrentino, the reality star from the TV hit "The Jersey Shore," hadn't even been born yet. They could have made millions!

And what makes it even more of a challenge is when you are a two-time divorcee. You get introduced to someone, and you can see the wheels spinning around in their minds: "*Really*? *Two* divorces. I wonder what's the matter … with *her*!"

But I learned a lesson as a child that has served me well over the years, and that is, "Beauty is only skin deep. It's what's inside that matters." And unfortunately, what's inside a lot of people going through divorce are many negative emotions: anger, fear, denial, and grief.

I think it's unfortunate that people still think of divorce as the end of their life, or that they'll never be able to move on. I have never thought of myself as a "Divorce Victim." Rather, I like to think of myself as a healthy person ... who was married to the wrong guys.

There are lots of different clubs we can belong to. For example, I belong to a health club, an alumnae club, a bridge club, golf club, and even The International Laurel & Hardy Society—Sons of the Desert. Now I'm a member of Divorcing Divas ... and I didn't even ask to join.

But it *is* a club, this Divorcing Divas "Club." It's not an exclusive club; it's a very inclusive club, probably because it includes nearly everyone on earth. Statistics say that more than 50 percent of marriages end in divorce. Who does that include? Our friends, our families, our caregivers, our employers. All of our lives have been or will be touched by divorce.

Because divorce has so permeated our society, it is up to all of us to help the new people just starting on this journey find a way to get back in to the mainstream of life. And I happen to think that one of the ways to do that is through laughter. In fact, I call it the world's best therapy!

Well, what exactly is "laughter"? *Webster* defines laughter as, "That which expresses amusement, mirth, contempt, fear by inarticulate explosive sounds which result from the forcing out of air, from the lungs, usually accompanied by convulsive, muscular movements, especially of the face."

Whew. If I didn't know better, I'd swear that is a great description of what I looked like when I was listening to my ex-husband's deposition!

George Burns, who lived to a ripe old age of 100 used to say, "Laughter prevents hardening of the attitudes!"

And perhaps you read the book *Anatomy of an Illness* by the famous author, Norman Cousins. When diagnosed with a terminal illness, he turned to laughter and attributed it to putting him in remission.

People are the only creatures on earth who can celebrate the joy of being alive. Laughter flings open the shutters and lets the sunshine in. A shared gift of laughter is a priceless gift to the spirit. And it's a great "poke in the eye" to the adversity people getting divorced have to experience every single day.

The Games People Play

*"I accept life unconditionally. Life holds so much—
so much to be so happy about always.
Most people ask for happiness on condition.
Happiness can be felt only if you don't set conditions."*

– Arthur Rubinstein

It hasn't been easy finding the humor in all that I went through. My psychologist said to me, "Christine, one day you will start to grieve. But it won't be for the loss of your husband. It will be for what you have endured."

Having been a survivor so many times in my life, it didn't take much for me to start digging myself out of the enormous hole I had dug for myself. The humor started coming back when I created a game I play with myself called "The Clue Phone's Ringing ... It's for You!" If I look back on hundreds of incidents that happened before I even married Mr. Wonderful, I realize I have no one to blame but myself. I had heard of "screen envy." You know, when you look at your computer monitor or the size of your television set and think, "Yeah, I could sure use a new one. A bigger one. A better one."

I now have phone envy. The Clue Phone had literally fallen off the wall from all the ringing! But I'm not sure I could have found a newer, bigger, or better one than the one ringing with the clues Mr. Wonderful left along the way.

Let's take the very first trip we took together, months after we were engaged. It happened to be to the Master's in Augusta, Georgia. Being an avid golfer, I thought I had died and gone to heaven. This was a dream come true to see the tournament and experience the ambiance of Augusta!

Since the weather back in Minnesota was still a little shaky that time of year, I asked Mr. Wonderful if he would like to bring his golf clubs to Georgia and play a round of golf. "Are you a golfer?" I had asked on that

The Clue Phone's Ringing

first twelve-hour date of ours, only a few months prior. "Oh, yes, I'm a *great* golfer. I've had two holes in one!" he bragged. Perfect. I set up a round of golf at a very prestigious course between Augusta and Atlanta. We'd play on our way back to the airport.

On the day of our round of golf, we paid $300 in greens fees and were told it was a "Members Only" course, so we'd be paired with members. A very nice, older couple greeted us on the first tee and said they'd be our hosts for the day.

On the first hole, each of them teed-up the ball and hit it straight down the middle. "My golf swing's a little rusty, living in Minnesota, but let me give this a try," I said. Lucky me. I found the fairway.

Mr. Wonderful teed-up the ball and proceeded to hit it dead left into the woods. At the second hole, the same thing happened. All three of us were straight down the middle. Mr. Wonderful might have killed a deer with his drive.

On the third hole, the three of us repeated our drives right down the center. When Mr. Wonderful's third drive careened dead left into the woods, he took his driver and slammed it into the ground so hard and so many times that the head broke off!

He picked up the head and tried to kick it into the woods, slipping and falling right on his butt. He stood up, picked the head up again and kicked it into the woods.

I turned to look at our hosts through my peripheral vision, too shocked to turn my entire head. Their mouths were wide open, and I realized that mine was, too. Mr. Wonderful jumped into the cart and announced, "I'm not playing anymore."

Clue Phone's Ringing ... It's for You:
MAY HAVE ABUSIVE TENDENCIES!

Let's take the time I first discovered Mr. Wonderful's internet surfing habits. It wasn't too difficult: he'd get online at night while I was sleeping, and in the morning when I'd awake, pop-up images of naked women would fill his computer screen. Confronting him with it, he actually wrote me a note that read, "I can honestly say it simply does not arouse me, and part of my curiosity is to understand why. The women look pretty ridiculous to me, and of course, not smart, which is very unattractive to me. So I've always wondered how someone could have the nerve to be photographed with no clothes on."

This from a man who could recite the names of every single Playboy Bunny from 1953 to the present Playmate of the Month, including their height, weight, and hair color (or lack thereof).

Clue Phone's Ringing ... It's For You:
MAY BE ADDICTED TO PORNO!!

The first time I took Mr. Wonderful to a party with me to meet my new friends, he pulled a traveling liquor case out of his closet and filled it with his own, hand-concocted combo: vodka, Campari, and grapefruit juice. He called this a "Blood Orange," and had even taught his favorite bartenders around town how to mix it. When he stepped into my friend's loft with his liquor cabinet in tow, my friend said to me, "Chris, there's something not right about a man who brings his own liquor with him."

Clue Phone's Ringing ... It's For You: MAY BE AN ALCOHOLIC!!!

I had moved in with Mr. Wonderful, but we weren't married yet. I always thought it was strange that I'd find bundles of unopened bills and invoices from everyplace—from the telephone company to the Mercedes dealership where he leased his car—stuffed into drawers. One night, while we were sleeping, Mercedes repossessed his car from the parking garage in the high-rise apartment complex where we were living! Still clueless when Mr. Wonderful blamed it on the dealership, I was informed that it would make sense for us just to drive one car. "We'll save rent on the extra parking space, gas, maintenance, and insurance." Made sense to me.

The only problem, however, happened shortly thereafter when we got into an argument. I actually slept in our guest room that night. When I woke, got dressed and went to find *my* car keys for *my* car, they were gone. Not only were the keys gone, my car was gone, too! Mr. Wonderful had hid the car in the neighborhood so that I wouldn't be able to leave.

Clue Phone's Ringing ... It's For You:
MAY BE FINANCIALLY UNSTABLE, MEAN, AND CRUEL. (Yeah, this one should have been enough by itself!!!!)

Then there was the time, only weeks before our wedding when we decided to go see Mr. Wonderful's mother. She was in her 80s and had hip problems that were going to prevent her from coming to our ceremony. She was a recovering alcoholic, who had been through treatment when she was 50 years old, and she and I got along famously.

As she put us in our rented car to head back to the airport on our final day visiting her, she put each of her hands on my shoulders, looked me squarely in the eyes and said, "Christine, he's *your* problem now!"

The Clue Phone's Ringing ... It's For You:
EVEN HIS MOTHER WARNED YOU! (GET OUT NOW!!!!!)

"I See," Says the Blind Woman

"A woman has got to love a bad man once or twice in her life, to be thankful for a good one."

– Marjorie Kinnan Rawlings

Perhaps there were clues being left for you, too. BIG CLUES. If you want to know if the phone's ringing for *you*, see if you can identify any of these general behaviors:

- He no longer has a tan line.
- He has discovered manscaping.
- He hired a personal trainer.
- His underwear no longer has skid marks.
- He actually went out and bought his own underwear: silk boxers.
- He tells you he has to go look at a piece of property. At 9:30pm.
- He tells you he is working late. But his response when you ask him why he didn't answer the phone at 10:00pm was, "I couldn't hear the phone because it was on night bell."
- He tells you he's started playing golf. He doesn't own any golf clubs.
- He bought new cologne.
- He decides to wash the windows without you having to ask.
- He went out for the Sunday paper. He didn't come back until Wednesday.
- His cell phone requires a password to unlock the keypad.
- He has a new email address, LinkedIn account, Facebook page, etc.
- He showers frequently.
- He has a new hairstyle or clothing (that he bought himself).

"I See," Says the Blind Woman

- He drops off and picks up his own dry cleaning.
- He argues less and agrees more.
- He has late and "emergency" meetings or unexpected travel extensions.
- He has new friendships (male or female).
- He has decided to take up horse-back riding.
- He has unexplained credit cards charges to places like "Snow Bunnies."
- You go to the doctor and discover you have an STD.
- He looks too good to be true.

Great Day to Be Alive ...

*"In three words I can sum up everything
I've learned about life: It goes on."*

– Robert Frost

I'm divorced, finally, and it has been well over two years since that day I took back my life. It was two years full of pain and sorrow, fear and anxiety, yet joy and liberation, peace and contentment also had their place. I miss his kids, and the times of good conversation. I grieved more about having to sell my beloved home than I did for the loss of my husband. And as with all things in life, I now ask myself, "What was I to learn from that experience, and how might I do things differently?"

Why don't we answer the Clue Phone when it rings? I think there are numerous reasons: love, affection, security, trust. "Ignorance is bliss," they say. I think I fell in love with the fantasy of who I "thought" Mr. Wonderful was instead of who he really is. Perhaps I thought I could "change" him. I think I was too embarrassed, having left my first marriage, to admit that I had made a mistake by hooking up with Mr. Wonderful. And I didn't have the confidence in myself that I could survive being on my own at the time. After all, I had never lived alone. I went from high school to college dorm, to sorority, to houses with girls, to a 29-year marriage to life with Mr. Wonderful. And at all times, at least one of our children was living with us. What would it be like to live completely alone?

Since I didn't pick up the receiver when the Clue Phone rang, it left a voicemail message for me: Don't do this alone. Get an Order of Protection against him. So I did—two days after filing for divorce.

I learned in that first year of legal separation that Mr. Wonderful probably had a drinking problem and a history of abuse going all the way back to high school. I heard from reliable sources that I wasn't the first woman he had hit. I learned after the fact that there was a record of abuse against him at a health club in the high-rise apartment he had lived in, when he was turned down for membership at my country club. As far as I can tell, he hasn't paid his taxes for two years, including the year I filed for divorce so the government has put a lien on his bank account. He got stopped for a DUI, but paid it off with community service. He was sued again by ex-wife #2 for over $400,000 in unpaid child support and alimony. But there was one thing he did do, and quickly: he found another girlfriend.

People like Mr. Wonderful can't live alone. They could never live with themselves, in isolation; if they did, they might have to acknowledge the destruction they've caused along the way. I feel sorry for his girlfriend, but know that as it was for me, this is her journey now.

I would do a lot of things differently in the future. The husband of one of my best friends tells me that if I ever get serious with another man, he's running a credit check, a police report, and asking for the guy's medical records and first-born child! Because if I had just done those things, I would have learned that four days before I met Mr. Wonderful, he had spent a night in jail. It's all right there in the public legal records of the Government Center.

I understand the pain that goes in to making decisions about divorce. It's never easy and it's never just about any one thing. I learned the biggest lesson in life, not from my battle with cancer or from facing two divorces, but from watching my youngest brother, James.

We should all have a James in our lives.

There are many things that can help us get through times of adversity: faith, hope, family, friendships, passion, purpose, and laughter. But perhaps there is nothing more powerful than the power of positive thinking that motivates us to continue, no matter what type of challenges we are facing.

My parents were told that my youngest brother, James, born with a congenital kidney defect, would never live to be ten years old. By the age of five, he had undergone twenty-three major surgeries.

James was seven when my mother was diagnosed with her breast cancer and eleven when *she* died. But he miraculously managed to go on living with my father, until the night before Dad was scheduled to retire from his thirty-year medical practice. It was New Year's Eve, and my father died of a massive heart attack.

The Clue Phone's Ringing

Within days of my father's death, James had total kidney failure and went on dialysis. I've often equated it to those stories we've all read: two people, who've lived together all of their lives, and then one passes away, and then shortly after, the other.

And yet James miraculously managed to stay on dialysis for seven years, and reached his thirty-fourth birthday. Three weeks after his birthday, I got a call that he was in the hospital.

"Christine, you won't believe what happened to me. I was just walking around my apartment, and my hip broke. They've put a pin in it, and I'll be in the hospital for awhile doing some physical therapy."

Two weeks later, came the second phone call.

"Christine, you *really* won't believe what happened to me *this* time! I was just lying in my hospital bed and my *other* hip broke! So they've had to do double hip-replacement surgery, and I'll be in the hospital for awhile longer doing my physical therapy."

The third phone call arrived ten days later.

"OK, Christine. You need to sit down for this one. I'm in the hospital, doing my physical therapy. I put all of the weight of my upper body on my crutches, and my elbow just shattered and broke."

"So, Chris, they've done a complete medical workup on me, and they've uncovered a brain aneurism and a tumor the size of a baseball on my pituitary gland."

I was in the middle of my chemotherapy and radiation when all of this was going on, and I truly had to stop and think to myself, "If that were *me*… after *everything* he's been through …I would just want them to take me out in the backyard and shoot me! What more could possibly happen to this young man?"

Well, they operated on the brain aneurism. They put him on some medication that shrunk the tumor, and it was benign. He got through all of his physical therapy. He was actually discharged from the hospital!

And five days after he was discharged, James got a phone call that after all of these years, they had finally found a match for his kidney.

So, seventeen years ago, my brother underwent a successful kidney transplant. And on the night of his surgery, I put in a call to USC Hospital in southern California. I didn't know if he'd be coherent or if they'd even let me speak to him.

But they patched me through, and the first words out of his mouth were, "*Christine, isn't this a great day to be alive?*"

And I knew right then, that if someone who had been through that much adversity could find the *strength* to *fight* and *go on,* that we *all* have that inside of us.

You know, we *all* have "things" going on in our lives. It doesn't have to be cancer or kidney failure. It could be another form of chronic illness. It could be side effects from the treatments we had to save our lives.

It could be our divorce; the loss of our job; the death of a loved one; environmental catastrophes.

We *all* have "things" going on in our lives, and we can't always change that "thing" in our life. I can never go back and change the fact that "I GOT DIVORCED … TWICE!"

There is one thing we can change and *do* something about: our attitude, and how we chose to deal with that "thing" on a go-forward basis.

James has truly been my inspiration and a gift to me and everyone he's touched. Who is *your* inspiration?

Keep on Movin' On! Top Ten Tips for Divorcing Divas

"The rung of the ladder was never meant to rest upon, but only to hold a woman's foot long enough to enable her to put the other somewhat higher."

– Thomas Henry Huxley

Some of you reading this book may not be the one who filed for divorce. I know that I am writing from a place of strength, being the one who initiated the proceedings. There's a difference. I get it.

I think there is a different kind of pain if you find out that your spouse has left you for a younger version of yourself. Or that he decided he needed to "Go find himself." Or he just simply took off one day and never came back. The grief must be overwhelming.

If some of you reading this book are also in abusive relationships, my psychologist told me to put together a "Safety Net." In it, you should have access to separate funds in the form of a checking or accessible savings account. You should have several extra sets of clothes. You should have an extra set of keys to the car and the house. You should be prepared to call 911. Then put all these things in a safe place like over at a friend's house that the abuser doesn't know about, or who lives far enough away that the abuser won't visit or intimidate or try to find you there once you leave.

When I told the psychologist that I had all those things put together, she looked me in the eye and said, "Christine, that's why I'm scared for you. Because you are *not* scared. You're in total denial that the abuse can and will happen again."

So how *do* you start moving forward? First, take this simple quiz. Get a grip on where you currently stand:

Keep on Movin' On! Top Ten Tips for Divorcing Divas

My current status is …

- ☐ Miserably Married …
- ☐ Blindsided by Divorce!
- ☐ My Boots are Walking!
- ☐ Will this Ever End?
- ☐ The Ink is Drying!
- ☐ Landed on Two Feet!

Now, knowing your status, and where you need to be (the last on that list!), follow these **Top Ten Tips for Divorcing Divas:**

1.) **Don't panic.** It's always OK in the end; if it's not OK, it's not the end. While divorce might seem like the end of the world, there is a reason for the divorce. So in the "end," you will have a better life.

2.) **Take four steps forward:** speak with an attorney/mediator, a financial planner, a realtor, and a psychologist. These four people can help you get moving in the right direction.

3.) **Surround yourself with supportive friends and family.** In adverse situations, you always learn who your friends are, and who they aren't. Leave behind the ones who are not supportive. Embrace the ones who are.

4.) **Realize that your life will never be the same.** That doesn't mean you won't have a good life—a *better* life. It just means it will be different. The sooner you can embrace your divorce, the sooner you will be able to move forward.

5.) **Research all the possibilities.** Read books, visit the internet, and listen to tapes on the topic of divorce, but also on topics such as fear, serenity, hope, and overcoming obstacles.

6.) **Do something special for yourself.** Treat yourself to something that will make you feel pampered: a massage, a change in hair color, buy a new outfit, or take a trip.

7.) **Don't be your own enemy.** Instead, ask yourself, "What am I supposed to learn from this marriage, and how might I do things differently in the future?"

8.) **Remember: YOU are the source of your happiness,** not somebody else.

9.) **Learn to forgive.** Harboring negative feelings will only slow down the progress of moving forward. Gather the tools and skills to find forgiveness through your church/synagogue, counseling, books and tapes, family and friends.

10.) **Don't forget to laugh!** Laughter is still the best medicine!

Remember: It's not the end … it's the beginning!

And now, speaking of laughter, how do you know if *you* are a Divorcing Diva? Simple. See if you recognize yourself in this next chapter. At the very least, have some good laughs!

You Might Be a Divorcing Diva If …

You Might Be a Divorcing Diva If ...

You opted for the silver instead of the flat screen TV.

You "forgot" your lingerie when moving out.

You Might Be a Divorcing Diva If ...

You let him have the used silk sheets ... and the mattress!

You sold all of your gold jewelry (from him) and went to Mexico with the girls.

You're a Super Diva if you went with your new love interest!

You Might Be a Divorcing Diva If ...

You got your belly button pierced before going to Mexico.

You Might Be a Divorcing Diva If ...

You suffered thru the "stress and anxiety diet" then wore new size six skinny jeans to school conferences!

You threw away your Mom panties and bought a thong!

You no longer have a tan line.

You Might Be a Divorcing Diva If ...

You used your ex's credit card points to buy a pair of Jimmy Choos.

A Super Diva if you wore them on a date!

You went back to your maiden name.

A Super Diva if your maiden name was Dicke.

You just discovered that "Brazilian" is not only a nationality.

You Might Be a Divorcing Diva If …

You burned your Unity Candle in the kids' jack-o-lantern.

You Might Be a Divorcing Diva If ...

You had a headache for fourteen years!

You sent a thank you note to the "other woman."

You Might Be a Divorcing Diva If ...

You moved the kitty litter box into his closet.

You Might Be a Divorcing Diva If…

You let him have the cat that used to pee in the plants.

You fought for sole custody of the dog.

A Super Diva if you won.

You kept the Lexus and gave him the mini-van.

A Super Diva if you let him have the jumper cables!

You Might Be a Divorcing Diva If ...

You had no intention of dividing the All-Clad cookware.

You decided to become an author after the divorce.

A Super Diva if Hollywood wants the movie rights.

You Might Be a Divorcing Diva If ...

You have already contacted Sandra Bullock to play you in the movie.

A Super Diva if she wins an Oscar!

You spent $55,478 in legal fees and $321 replacing your grannie panties, but believe regaining your sanity is priceless!

You know the definitions of "cougar" and "MILF."

A Super Diva if you are one or both!

You Might Be a Divorcing Diva If ...

You chose the china and crystal instead of the lawn mower

You found out how to log in to his Match.com account.

A Super Diva if you had the nerve to "update" his profile!

You gave him back his love notes and cards.

A Super Diva if you wrote a note saying, "Hope you can use these with your new internet girlfriends," and meant it.

You Might Be a Divorcing Diva If ...

You kept the Halloween decorations, but gave him the wedding video.

A Super Diva if your kids are over thirteen.

You Might Be a Divorcing Diva If ...

You prefer your BOB (battery operated boyfriend) over sex with your ex!

You Might Be a Divorcing Diva If ...

Your "date night" is code for sharing a bottle of wine with BOB.

You Might Be a Divorcing Diva If...

Your virginity was restored during your marriage

You Might Be a Divorcing Diva If ...

You could have been nominated for an Oscar in the category of "Best Actress ..."

You had a special nickname for your ex (such as "Itty Bitty") so you could talk about him under a veil of secrecy ...

You Might Be a Divorcing Diva If ...

You prefer the dead brown grass on the other side of the fence.

You Might Be a Divorcing Diva If …

Your "kid-free" weekends are your silver lining!

You decided his ability to fix your computer wasn't worth the headaches you get when it breaks down.

You've become best friends with the woman who bought your house from you.

A Super Diva if she's getting divorced, too.

You found Viagra in his brief case.

A Super Diva if you've never stepped foot in his office.

You think impotence is a gift from God.

A Super Diva if you "accidently" flushed his Viagra during worship.

You Might Be a Divorcing Diva If ...

You'd rather run the snow blower than ... never mind!

You've decided that six degrees of separation is not far enough!

You encouraged his departure by sabotaging the cable box.

A Super Diva if you sabotaged his computer.

You hid the T.V. remote in the washer knowing he'd never find it.

You Might Be a Divorcing Diva If ...

You feel the day your divorce was final is outshined only by the birth of your children.

You yelled "Mulligan" in your sleep on the night of your 2nd anniversary.

A Super Diva if you told him, "No. I don't want to touch your balls."

You took the new washer and dryer with you when you moved.

A Super Diva if you took the detergent and Bounce.

You started negotiating your divorce settlement in your mind on your wedding anniversary over a bottle of wine.

You finally accepted that the economy was not going to recover quickly enough to warrant putting off the inevitable.

A Super Diva if you talked to your realtor before you talked to him about the divorce.

You signed up for a full year of dance lessons.

A Super Diva if you used his credit card.

You Might Be a Divorcing Diva If ...

You sent him flowers when the divorce was final.

You have your Home Page set to MeetingMillionaires.com.

You threw out all the perfumes he bought you.

A Super Diva if you ordered No. 1 from Imperial Majesty at $2,150 an ounce ... using his credit card.

You traded out the chandelier in your dining room before you put the house up for sale.

A Super Diva if he didn't notice.

You couldn't stop staring at the butt crack of the gorgeous Brazilian handyman who came to your new place to put up the chandelier.

You don't think your new King size bed is large enough.

You kept the Bvlgari shampoo and conditioner and let him have all those sample sizes from the Holiday Inn.

You've now tried Botox.

A Super Diva if everyone tells you, "You've never looked better."

You finally let your hair grow longer.

A Super Diva if you dyed it a different color.

You Might Be a Divorcing Diva If…

You've finally shot your career round in golf.

A Super Diva if you did it using his balls.

You let him have the sofa, chairs, tables, and lamps because just looking at them reminded you of him.

A Super Diva if you found even better ones on Craigslist.

You've got BUY & TRADE Your Gold Jewelry on speed dial!

You Might Be a Divorcing Diva If ...

You own stock in Pure Romance.

Two Men and a Truck is on stand-by.

You've taken up a new career as a pole dancer.

A Super Diva if you're going to audition for the Victoria's Secret Fashion Show.

You got him a Shih Tzu so he would become a "Chick Magnet."

You can finally admit that your mother was right about him.

A Super Diva if you can admit *his* mother was right about him!

You Might Be a Divorcing Diva If ...

You gave him back to his mother!

Taking the High Road

"There is in every true woman's heart a spark of heavenly fire, which lies dormant in the broad daylight of prosperity; but which kindles up, and beams and blazes in the dark hour of adversity."

– Washington Irving

Settlements are never what you were expecting. In my case, after eight rejected Proposals for Settlement, two unsuccessful attempts at mediation (he got up and walked out of the first session), and lots of dollars spent, we discovered four days before trial that Mr. Wonderful's second ex-wife had been successful in freezing all of his assets. In the end, I walked away.

But there are other ways of being a graceful Divorcing Diva. Perhaps you might recognize yourself here, and if not today, perhaps someday.

You Might Be a Divorcing Diva If …

You Might Be a Divorcing Diva If ...

You prefer living alone to living a lie.

You finally understand that you make your own happiness.

You successfully negotiated your divorce settlement without too many nasty tactics, and a fairly low level of conflict.

You believe that what doesn't drag you under, makes you stronger.

You were wise enough to know that happiness and emotional well-being is far more important than worrying about the "stigma" of getting a divorce ... or two!

You discovered resilience, strength, and confidence you never knew you had.

A Super Diva if you learned to love and forgive yourself and walk into your future better than you were before!

You Might Be a Divorcing Diva If ...

You understand now that your children will be better off in two happy homes than one conflicted home.

You believe that being a good Mom starts with being good to yourself.

You understand that a "good enough" Mom is sometimes exactly that.

A Super Diva if you can apply the same theory to Dad.

You make it easy for your children to maintain ties with his extended family.

A Super Diva if you tell your kids it's "OK" to like his new significant other.

Despite how you feel about him, you encourage your children to maintain a close relationship with their Dad.

A Super Diva if you occasionally say nice things about him.

Remove Foot from Mouth

"I cannot help believing that the world will be a better and a happier place when people are praised more and blamed less; when we utter in their hearing the good we think and also gently intimate the criticisms we hope may be of service."

– Francis E. Willard

OK. So now you're moving forward. But people say the darndest things! Friends and family mean well, they truly do. But often the words that come out of their mouths seem hurtful, discouraging, or insensitive. It's good to reach out to people going through divorce: it helps them feel supported, that they are not alone, and that life will, indeed, go on. But do so with care.

Here are the Divorcing Divas Top Ten Things You Should Never Say to Someone Going through Divorce, and some valuable suggestions on how to say things differently:

1.) **"Don't worry. You'll find a better man (or woman)!"** That's what everyone said to me after my first divorce. But that isn't exactly what happened, as you can tell from my story. A better thing to say would be, for example, "I'm sorry things didn't work out for you. He obviously wasn't the right person for you. At some point, if you want someone in your life, I'm sure you will meet a really nice person. And if that isn't the direction you want to go, you have lots of good friends who are here to support you." Defining "better" leads you to believe that you didn't make a wise choice in the first place, which I obviously didn't (Now I can laugh!). That comment also implies that you "have to have a man/woman in your life to be whole."

2.) Or another is, **"Everything will be all right."** No one has a way to know if everything will be all right, and you certainly don't want to hear that from someone who simply doesn't know. For some people going through divorce, things couldn't be worse. A better thing to say would be, "I haven't been through this journey myself, and I'm sure it's going to be difficult. But please know that I'm here for you in any way I can help, and you can always feel free to lean on me."

3.) Or, **"I know how you feel."** Hmm ... if they've been through a divorce, they may have "an" understanding, but unless they were married to the person I described in this book, they have no idea what my experience was like. Unless someone has experienced that, they really don't know how you feel. A better response would be, "I think of you often, Christine, and even hold you in my prayers. If you ever need someone to talk to, I'm here to listen."

4.) **"I never liked him/her anyway."** Knowing that all of your best friends or family members didn't like your spouse from the get-go is not comforting. The big question here is, "Why didn't you say something during our marriage? Perhaps your feelings might have been a clue that there was something wrong to begin with." A kinder way of letting someone know you didn't care for their spouse would be to say, "There seemed to be some differences, and I'm sure that is one of the reasons you left/they left." Or even better would be: "It was painful for me to watch how you were treated during your marriage, and I worried about you as I saw you disappear during that time." Another? "It was hard for me to like him/her because of the way he/she treated you."

5.) **"I had heard rumors that he/she was _____ (fill in the blank) cheating, drinking too much, gambling, etc."** There are lots of debates over whether or not a good friend should tell another the things that are circulating about their spouse. In the end, honesty is the best policy. Try to broach the subject with words such as, "I'm one of your best friends, and what I have to say to you may be difficult for you to hear. I don't know if it is true, but I'm just letting you know what I'm hearing about your spouse." Then let them make the decision if they want to take any action regarding the "rumors." It's more difficult to think that a good friend or family member knew information before you did and never told you than it is to hear something that you can investigate.

6.) **"Take him/her for all he/she is worth!"** Anyone who has been through or is facing divorce knows that divorce doesn't come cheap. Time is money in the divorce industry, and you would be better off sitting down with a good financial planner, and perhaps a mediator to figure out "What do I need to survive, and then thrive?" No one needs to take their spouse to the cleaners. Children may be involved, and college educations may be in your family's future. The harder you fight the battle, the more money you both lose … to attorneys. Be reasonable.

7.) **"I never knew what you saw in him/her anyway. You were much _____ (fill in the blank) prettier/handsome, smarter, more talented, etc."** Beauty is in the eye of the beholder. Telling someone that the person they were married to was not attractive to them doesn't mean that you didn't think he/she was the most handsome man/beautiful woman in the world. Instead, say something like, "You are such a bright woman. When you're ready, I'm confident you'll meet another person who is just as smart as you are."

8.) **"The divorce was your fault, you know. You were _____ (fill in the blank) never home, always out with your friends, living your own life, etc."** Divorce is never the fault of one person. It takes two in a marriage. Putting blame on someone is harmful and shameful. Say instead, "I know it takes two to make a marriage. You don't have to share with me, if you're not comfortable, why the marriage fell apart, but I wish you both happiness."

9.) **"You need to get out there and start dating again!"** No, I don't. Maybe you need time to work on what you feel your role was in the demise of the marriage. Maybe you need to spend time rebuilding trust. Maybe you need to spend time with your girlfriends/boyfriends. If and when you decide you want to start dating again, you will let your friends know. In the meantime, offer to go out with the divorcee and go to movies, bowling, dinner, etc. Having company and friends to support you is extremely important.

10.) **"Don't worry, the kids will survive. Kids are so resilient!"** If children are involved, this could be your biggest worry. You have turned their lives upside down. This comment may come across as flippant, like "Ah, kids adjust. They'll be OK." Yet at the time, you can't imagine that their lives will be unaffected. Instead, say something like, "I know how hard this must be on your children. If I can help you in any way by driving them to Scouts/sports/appointments, let me know. I care so much about you, and your kids are important to me, too."

So, what is the one thing you should always say to someone going through divorce?

Don't forget to laugh! It may feel like you will never laugh again. But you will ... when you're ready. Humor comes to people in lots of different forms and timing is a very individual thing. A nice way to introduce humor into the life of a divorcee would be to say, "When you are ready, I would love to take you to this funny movie/play/production" or "I have this very funny book for you, if you feel you are up to reading something with humor in it. One day, you will laugh again."

Don't Forget to Laugh!

"Blessed is she who has learned how to laugh at herself, for she shall never cease to be entertained."

– John Bowell

I have learned many, many things about being a two-time divorcee. But the thing I've learned the best, is that everyone who has been through this horrible ordeal is a hero. Each of you has a story to share, and if we could fit all of your stories in this book, every one of them would pull at our heartstrings if we let it.

My story is no different than any of yours. I am very blessed. I am very grateful. I've found complete peace and contentment. I'd like to thank all of you for listening to my story, and I'd like to close with a poem I wrote called *Don't Forget to Laugh!*

> My life was perfect, or so it seemed
> It far surpassed what I had dreamed.
> My boys were healthy, ages twelve and nine,
> My twenty-year marriage was doing fine.
> I had more friends than I could see;
> For a brand new house, I held the key.
> I'd cracked that "glass ceiling," for which I had fought;
> Life doesn't get better than this, I thought.
> One day, but years later, it became crystal clear.
> It can't be the thing that so deeply I fear.
> I knew as I drove to my lawyer that noon
> My life would be changing, profoundly and soon.
> An Agreement was drawn right on the spot
> We hoped it'd go quickly, this divorce that I sought.
> The wait for resolution was frightening and long.
> What had I done for my life to go wrong?
> I'll never forget that one day in December
> The words as she spoke them, I hardly remember.

The Clue Phone's Ringing

"You're divorced now," she said. Her words rang in my ears
And before I could stop, I cried buckets of tears.
The anger, confusion, denial, and grief
To die and escape would seem such a relief.
Then I looked all around me; the things that I had.
To fight and continue could not be that bad.
I tackled my journey like nobody could,
I did everything specialists told me I should.
Friends, family, psychologist all gave me support
Yet despite all their gestures, I felt something was short.
I realized that laughter is just what I need
And once I had found it, I planted the seed.
It may not fix marriage or cure a disease
But it will take your mind off and give it a tease.
So if you're a divorcee, survivor, or friend
And you want to help win this race, in the end,
Remember that "ATTITUDE" is the key to success.
A good one can do it for you, is my guess.
So nothing is ever quite perfect, it seems.
Our lives take many paths and often sway from our dreams.
Look around and rejoice in the things that you have
Oh, yes, one last reminder: Don't forget to laugh!

The Clue Phone's Ringing ... It's for You!

Resources

Have You Heard About ... ?

Books:

After the Ball: A Woman's Tale of Reclaiming Happily Ever After, by Barb Greenberg

Contemplating Divorce: A Step-By-Step Guide to Deciding Whether to Stay or Go, by Susan Pease Gadoua

Crazy Time: Surviving Divorce and Building a New Life, by Abigail Trafford

Cutting Loose: Why Women Who End Their Marriages Do So Well, by Ashton Applewhite

Divorce & Money: How to Make the Best Financial Decisions During Divorce, by Violet Woodhouse

Divorce for Dummies, by John Ventura & Mary Reed

Heartburn, by Nora Ephron

Helping Your Kids Cope with Divorce the Sandcastles Way, by M. Gary Neuman and Patricia Romanowski

He's History, You're Not: Surviving Divorce After 40, by Erica Manfred and Tina Tessina, PhD

How to Avoid the Divorce from Hell, and Dance Together at Your Daughter's Wedding, by Sue Talia

I Remember Nothing, by Nora Ephron

Make Your Divorce Cost You Less by Deborah Gibson and can be downloaded at: www.makeyourdivorcecostyouless.com

Making Divorce Work: 8 Essential Keys to Resolving Conflict & Rebuilding Your Life, by Diana Mercer & Katie Jane Wennechuk

The Clue Phone's Ringing

Mom's House, Dad's House: A Complete Guide for Parents Who Are Separated, Divorced, or Living Apart, by Isolina Ricci

Nolo's Essential Guide to Divorce, by Emily Doskow

Texas – Land of the Big Hair: Big Money Divorce Texas Style!, by Sonya Bernhardt and Good & Light

The Divorce Organizer & Planner, by Brette Sember

The Good Divorce, by Constance R. Ahrons

The Truth About Children and Divorce: Dealing with the Emotions So You and Your Children Can Thrive, by Robert E. Emery

The Unexpected Legacy of Divorce, by Judith S. Wallerstein

The Woman's Book of Divorce: 101 Ways to Make Him Suffer Forever & Ever, by Christine Gallagher

We're Still Family: What Grown Children Have to Say About Their Parents' Divorce, by Isolina Ricci

What Every Woman Should Know About Divorce and Custody, by Gayle Rosenwald Smith, JD, and Sally Abrahms

Your Divorce Pocket Guide, by Linda C. Senn

360 Degrees Back to Life: A Litigant's Humorous Perspective on Divorce, by Vandana Shah

National Organizations

Alcoholics Anonymous – www.aa.org

American Academy of Matrimonial Lawyers – www.aaml.org

American Academy of Child & Adolescent Psychiatry – www.aacap.org

American Association for Marriage and Family Therapy – www.aamft.org

Association of Family and Conciliation Courts – www.afccnet.org

Divorce Central – www.divorcecentral.com

Resources Page

International Academy of Collaborative Professionals – www.collaborativepractice.com

Kids' Turn Central – www.kidsturncentral.com

National Coalition Against Domestic Violence – www.ncadv.org

National Foundation for Credit Counseling – www.nfcc.org

The National Domestic Violence Hotline (24-hour hotline): (800)799-SAFE (7233) or (800)787–3224

WomensLaw.org – www.womenslaw.org

Internet and Social Media:

DivorceSupport.com – www.divorcesupport.com

HuffPostDivorce.com – www.huffingtonpost.com/divorce/

Mediate.com – www.Mediate.com

MeetUp.com – www.meetup.com

Planning for Parenting Time: Arizona's Guide for Parents Living Apart:

http://azcourts.gov/Portals/31/ParentingTime/PPWguidelines.pdf

Virginia's Spare the Child Video – http://www.vsb.org/site/sections/family/view/spare-the-child/

Services:

Our Family Wizard – www.ourfamilywizard.com

ShareKids.com – www.sharekids.com

Internet Keywords for Local Resources:

Divorce mediation or divorce mediators

Collaborative law or Cooperative law

Divorce attorneys

State Statutes on divorce, child support, alimony/spousal maintenance, property division

Do-it-yourself (pro se) divorce forms through your state court system

Divorce education classes

Products:

Divorce Shower Store – www.divorceshowerstore.com

Laughter: It's Good Therapy! (DVD) by Christine K. Clifford – www.divorcingdivas.net

Smashing Katie: A Perfectly Cheeky Breakup Boutique – www.smashingkatie.com

And Now For Some Unsolicited Advice: Moving Forward Into the Great Unknown

"There are very few certainties that touch us all in this mortal experience, but one of the absolutes is that we will experience hardship and stress at some point."

– Dr. James C. Dobson

My dear friend, Family Mediator and Parenting Specialist extraordinaire and fellow Divorcing Diva Amber Serwat helped me learn a lot about divorce. People are usually unprepared for the extent of the pain and the length of time it takes to recover from divorce. Some research indicates a recovery time of half the length of the marriage from start to finish. What can you expect? Certainly contradictory feelings and thoughts during your divorce. Understanding what you can and cannot control is important. Remember: you can only control your own behavior and reactions to your situation.

We all have family and friends who rally around us during times of crisis, and divorce is no exception. Although there is no doubt that a strong support network is vitally important, sometimes it is the people who love and care about us the most who unwittingly lead us astray with their good intentions. Your brother's wife's cousin who is a personal injury attorney is probably not the best choice for your divorce attorney… even if the service would be free. Same is true for your co-worker's best friend's "pit-bull" attorney who "won" her a large settlement… at the price of a small fortune. Each and every divorce is unique: what is true for one family may not be true for another. Generally speaking, divorce laws are fairly vague, which means the application and interpretation of the law vary widely, from state to state, county to county and even judge to judge. Referrals are an excellent place to *begin* searching for divorce professionals; however, you should not retain or hire a divorce professional until after your careful and thoughtful research and interviews confirm that the referred professional is indeed the best fit for your needs.

This is your life. Despite the disheartening and often overwhelming nature of a divorce—it is important to control your own journey. In order to complete your journey, you will likely need professional assistance, such as a mediator and/or attorney; therapist, CPA, financial planner, custody evaluator, parenting consultant, or other specialized expert. In addition to possessing the proper credentials, these experts must also be committed to serving and protecting *all* of your best interests; especially the best interests of your children and even your soon-to-be ex.

No one ever "wins" at divorce. Even if you prevail in a trial, you will likely experience a significant loss in another area of your life; be it financial, emotional, medical, or child related. The negative consequences and costs of the battle typically far outweigh the victory.

> *"Holding on to anger is like grasping a hot coal with the intent of throwing it at someone else; You are the one who gets burned."*
>
> – Gautama Siddhartha

Many Divorcing Divas begin their divorce journey with the goal and intent of being cooperative in order to save money and protect the children. Many discuss possible agreements with their husband at the kitchen table but despite their best efforts, they hit a road block because they did not know how to proceed, were unable to generate creative solutions, and/or were derailed by strong emotions that obstructed successful negotiations. It is typically at this point that many people seek professional assistance.

The type of assistance you seek determines the nature of your divorce journey and impacts everything from your financial security, mental, and physical health, to your children's emotional adjustment and well-being, and your long-term ability to parent effectively after divorce. Now is not the time for maliciousness or punishment as these motivations lead only to mutual suffering and wasted expense.

And Now For Some Unsolicited Advice

"The only cure for grief is action."
– G.H. Lewes

Key truths about divorce:

1. Regardless of process, most divorce cases settle prior to reaching trial.
2. You are the expert in your life.
3. You are capable of making fair and reasonable decisions about your future.
4. You have choices when deciding how to proceed with your divorce.
5. Self-determined agreements yield better results than imposed outcomes.

Steps to Success:

1. Thoughtfully consider how you want your future to unfold in the short and long term.
2. Educate yourself about different methods of divorce settlement.
3. Carefully interview professionals (attorneys, mediators, evaluators, etc.) prior to retaining their services.
4. Select a process that supports and encourages self-determination, provides timely resolution, and conserves financial resources.
5. Hire professionals who understand and will respect your needs and preferences including the needs and long-term well-being of your children.
6. Be actively involved in seeking self-determined outcomes and be fully engaged with your professionals; listen to their guidance but remember, *this is your life* and you are the one who has to live with the outcomes.
7. Understand *all* of the associated costs of a course of action before implementing it. Consider benefits (gains) compared to cost (losses) including: financial costs, time required, physical and emotional stress, as well as negative effects on children and/or parenting.
8. Speak up and address your concerns if you feel the process is not fulfilling your needs or is out of control.

9. Your professionals work for *you*. If after addressing your concerns with them directly, they are not responding to your needs or providing the type of service you want, hire another professional.

About the Author

All of us have read or heard stories about people who turn lemons into lemonade. It isn't often that we get the privilege of meeting such an individual.

Before her bout with breast cancer, **Christine Clifford** had definitely cracked the "glass ceiling." By age 40, she was Senior Executive Vice President for The SPAR Group, an international marketing firm in New York. Once the top salesperson in the multi-billion dollar retail services industry, Christine's accounts included Kmart, Toys "R" Us, Procter & Gamble, AT&T, Mattel Toys, and Revlon.

Diagnosed with breast cancer in December of 1994, Christine wrote six award-winning portrayals of her story in her books entitled *Not Now... I'm Having a No Hair Day!*, *Our Family Has Cancer, Too!* written especially for children, *Inspiring Breakthrough Secrets to Live Your Dreams*, *Cancer Has Its Privileges: Stories of Hope and Laughter*, *Your Guardian Angel's Gift* and *YOU, Inc. The Art of Selling Yourself.*

Christine is President and CEO of Divorcing Divas®, a company that hosts all-day educational conferences for people going through divorce. She is also CEO/President of The Cancer Club®, the world's largest producer of humorous and helpful products for people with cancer. She owns an anti-aging product distributorship, and is CEO of Christine Clifford Enterprises, a marketing and consulting firm in Minneapolis.

Featured in over 2,000 media hits, Christine appeared on *CNN Live* as "one of the world's leading authorities on the use of therapeutic humor."

Host of *The Christine Clifford Celebrity Golf Tournament*, Christine's inaugural event in 1998 raised over $100,000, making it the most successful first-year event in the history of the American Cancer Society. Christine's contribution has been over $1,000,000.

Christine earned her CSP designation (Certified Speaking Professional) from the National Speakers Association. Less than 550 people hold the CSP, putting Christine in the top 7% of professional speakers worldwide.

She has two sons, Tim & Brooks, and is grandmother to Siberian Husky, Skylar, in Minneapolis.

About the Illustrator

A native Minnesotan, **Jack Lindstrom** specializes in humorous illustrations for various print media—books, periodicals, and newspapers. For many years, he collaborated with William Wells to produce a daily comic strip, *Bull 'N' Bears* for United Feature Syndicate. He is also a partner in Finkstrom Productions specializing in greeting cards and humorous calendars.

Jack is married to his high school sweetheart, receives unsolicited advice from two grown children, and helps to spoil his three grandchildren whenever the opportunity presents itself ... which is often.

About Divorcing Divas®

"It's not the end ... It's the beginning!"

Divorcing Divas (www.DivorcingDivas.net), based in Minneapolis, Minnesota, was created by Christine Clifford in 2010 in response to her experience following her second divorce. Christine, who had now initiated two divorces in her life, realized that in doing so, she felt empowered, like a "bird out of a cage."

And yet as she spoke to friends and colleagues facing this journey, she found that many of them couldn't even get out of bed in the morning. They felt as if their feet were "stuck in cement."

How could she pass on the knowledge she had learned, and help others on this journey? She met a total stranger, Barb Greenberg, for a cup of coffee on the urging of a mutual friend. In a window seat over a two-hour conversation, sharing their stories of what they had been through, **Divorcing Divas** was born, a date was set for the first all-day conference, and the agenda was jotted down on a paper napkin!

Today, **Divorcing Divas** is a vital company offering all-day educational conferences dedicated to helping others as they transition through divorce to a new future.

Our Mission:

Divorcing Divas, LLC provides encouragement, inspiration, and empowerment to people going through the difficult process of divorce. Through support, education, resources, and hope, we show divorcees that they can find life—and a *good* life—on the other side.

About Divorcing Divas®

It is not our intention to be an "advocate" for divorce.
In some cases, divorce is the right decision.
Sometimes, it is not the right decision.
And sometimes, it is the only decision.
"It's not the end ... It's the beginning."

Christine Clifford is president and chief executive officer of Divorcing Divas, LLC. As a member of the National Speakers Association and a Certified Speaking Professional, Christine lectures and tours on behalf of many organizations internationally and is happy to share her story of finding hope and humor in divorce with you and your organization.

For more information about Divorcing Divas®, call (952)944-0639. Email us at:

Christine@DivorcingDivas.net . Or write:
Divorcing Divas, LLC®
PO Box 24747
Edina, MN 55424-0747

www.divorcingdivas.net

"It's not the end ... It's the beginning!"™

About The Cancer Club®

The Cancer Club.

"A shared gift of laughter is a priceless gift to the spirit."

– Christine Clifford

The Cancer Club, based in Minneapolis, Minnesota, was created by Christine Clifford in 1995 in response to her experience with breast cancer. Christine, whose mother died of breast cancer at the age of forty-two, found that during her own treatment, family and friends were supportive, but they also were careful to avoid humorous conversation or topics around her.

Needing a lift, Christine began to search for signs of humor in herself and her predicament. She found them daily. The more she laughed, the stronger she grew, and The Cancer Club® was born.

The critically acclaimed Cancer Club® is the first organization to offer hope and support to cancer patients, their families and friends through the healing power of humor. It serves as an international clearinghouse for people affected by cancer, offering inspirational gifts and providing information and resources through their website, www.cancerclub.com.

Cancer Club® products include all of Christine's books, including *Not Now ... I'm Having a No Hair Day!*, *Our Family Has Cancer, Too!* (written especially for children), *Cancer Has Its Privileges: Stories of Hope & Laughter*, *Inspiring Breakthrough Secrets to Live Your Dreams*, *Your Guardian Angel's Gift*, DVDs, custom jewelry, stuffed animals, ornaments, and more. A special DVD, *One Move at a Time! Exercise for Women Recovering from Breast Cancer Surgery*, was written, directed and produced by Christine Clifford.

Christine Clifford is president and chief executive officer of The Cancer Club®. As a member of the National Speakers Association and a Certified

About The Cancer Club®

Speaking Professional, Christine lectures and tours on behalf of many organizations internationally and is happy to share her stories of using humor to get through life's adversities with you and your organization.

For more information about The Cancer Club®, call (952)944-0639. Email us at: Christine@cancerclub.com. Or write:

The Cancer Club®
PO Box 24747
Edina, MN 55424-0747

www.cancerclub.com

Don't forget to laugh! ™

Other Books by Christine Clifford

Not Now ... I'm Having a No Hair Day: Humor & Healing for People with Cancer

Written by Christine Clifford
Illustrated by Jack Lindstrom
112 pages
ISBN 1-57025-120-7
Publication Date: August 1, 1996 (University of Minnesota Press)

Inspired by the author's experience with breast cancer, *Not Now ... I'm Having a No Hair Day!* is the first book of its kind to offer hope to cancer patients, their families and friends through the healing power of humor.

In her straightforward style, first-time author Christine Clifford, CSP paints a realistic picture of what it's like discover cancer, undergo surgery, and endure radiation and chemotherapy treatments. But unlike most cancer patients, she manages to find humor in herself and her predicament. Throughout the book, her moments of fear, frustration, uncertainty, love, and joy are captured by the gentle wit of illustrator Jack Lindstrom in 60 cartoons that reveal the vulnerability and strength of the human soul. Together, Clifford and Lindstrom show readers how the power of laughter and positive thinking go a long way toward promoting recovery and growth.

"... *No Hair Day!* is a wonderful book. Humor, that's the most important ingredient for facing the enemy–cancer. I had breast cancer in 1979–surgery, chemotherapy for a year. I'm sure it was laughter from God that saved me."
- Julie Harris, star of stage, screen, and television.

"I've always felt that humor is even better than chicken soup for the healing process. My friend Christine Clifford's book handles grave subject matter with sensitivity and warmth."
- Jim Davis, cartoonist and creator of Garfield™

"You are doing great work. I am inspired by your message."
- Jack Canfield, author of *Chicken Soup for the Soul*

Other Books by Christine Clifford

Our Family Has Cancer, Too!

Written by Christine Clifford
Illustrated by Jack Lindstrom
64 pages
ISBN 1-57025-144-4
Publication Date: October 1997 (University of Minnesota Press)

Christine has broken new ground once again with this book. With the help and insight of her son, Tim, Christine has explored the issues facing families when cancer becomes a part of life.

Author's Note to Children
Cancer isn't fair, but through it all, know you are loved ... and that you can help your family because you bring a special piece to the puzzle ... You!

Author's Note to Parents
When I was first diagnosed with cancer, I decided that in my family we would not waste any of the time we had together. I hope this book will encourage you to talk about the disease—but most of all, to truly live.

Complete with a glossary for children, Christine's book offers an opportunity for you and your family to learn and share feelings with each other about cancer and to answer the questions most kids have:
- What is cancer?
- What changes will happen to our family?
- What are the treatments like?
- How long will it take to get through the cancer experience?
- What do I tell my friends?

But most importantly, it teaches you how to laugh together! Once again, Clifford and Lindstrom show readers how the power of laughter and positive thinking go a long way toward promoting recovery and growth.

The Clue Phone's Ringing

Cancer Has Its Privileges: Stories of Hope and Laughter

Written by Christine Clifford
160 pages
ISBN 0-399-52776-1
Publication Date: May 2002 (Perigee)

Cancer survivor and founder of The Cancer Club®, Christine Clifford, CSP has been sharing her inspiring, humorous outlook on living with cancer with thousands of cancer patients and their families. Now she has gathered a collection of battlefield stories and anecdotes from her fellow survivors that go from the outright hilarious to the downright moving, and combined them with her own personal story of triumphant survival.

"A remarkable woman whose sense of humor became her best weapon against an often dehumanizing disease."
- Arnold Palmer, from the Introduction

"A book filled with what I call survival behavior. A meaningful life is built on love and laughter and this book shares both ... I recommend it to all those who have the desire to be survivors."
- Bernie Siegel, M.D., author of *Love, Medicine and Miracles*

"The perfect dose of medicine for anyone whose life has been touched by cancer."
- Michele Smith, Olympic gold medalist

"You don't have to have had cancer to be a survivor. Christine's inspirational and pathologically positive attitude should be shared by everyone who has faced adversity. God definitely has a plan for this woman."
-Larry Gatlin, Grammy Award winning singer/songwriter

Your Guardian Angel's Gift

Written by Christine Clifford
64 pages
ISBN 1-932458-30-1
Publication Date: August 1, 2005 (Bronze Bow Publishing)

You or someone you love, now or very soon, needs the message this book contains. As the title says, it is a gift. Almost all of us can remember the time, date, and place we were when we learned that we or someone we care about received bad news. Negative emotions filled our heads, feelings of denial, grief, anger, and fear. Following the initial shock, we turn to the one thing that makes us human—our will to survive, and then thrive.

Your Guardian Angel's Gift, a beautiful full-color gift book, is the perfect answer to this need. It has an unforgettable message of hope and encouragement that transcends life's challenges and goes straight to the heart of anyone facing adversity. After all, we all have a Guardian Angel up in heaven. Yours has sent a feather to the ground to let you know she's watching over you.

The Clue Phone's Ringing

Inspiring Breakthrough Secrets to Live Your Dreams

Co-Authored by Christine Clifford
224 pages
ISBN 1-890427-08-X
Publication Date: October 1, 2001

From the award-winning author of *Not Now ... I'm Having a No Hair Day!* and *Our Family Has Cancer, Too!* comes a book that will transform you to take action to live the life you've always dreamed of.
"If you believe in yourself, your product, your service, or your cause, anything is possible."
- Christine Clifford

North America's most inspiring authorities in personal and professional transformation reveal secrets, insights, and strategies that will empower you to break through your limitations and live your dreams.
In her straightforward style, author, Professional Speaker and President/CEO of The Cancer Club, Christine Clifford, CSP believes adversity can be the stepping-stone to living your dream. In the chapter, "The Blessings of Misfortune: Learn to Spin Straw into Gold," Christine will lead you through the steps that will help your dreams come true.

"Everyone wants to have a breakthrough now. This master teacher has, at long last, congealed her genius in this book. You can create phenomenal breakthroughs. Read it! Use it! Share it! And make your life a masterpiece."
- Mark Victor Hanson, co-creator, #1 *New York Times* best-selling series *Chicken Soup for the Soul*

"Here it is! This inspiring book is warm, witty and a wonderful way to clarify your heart's desire. If you follow its practical ideas, your whole life opens up before you like a summer sunrise."
- Brian Tracy, Author, *The 100 Absolutely Unbreakable Laws of Business Success*